Under Another Sky

An anthology of Commonwealth Poetry Prize winners

UNDER ANOTHER SKY

*An anthology of Commonwealth
Poetry Prize winners*

edited and introduced by
Alastair Niven

foreword by James Porter

CARCANET

First published in Great Britain 1987 by
Carcanet Press Limited
208-212 Corn Exchange Buildings
Manchester M4 3BQ

Carcanet
198 Sixth Avenue
New York, New York 10013

British Library Cataloguing in Publication Data

Under another sky : an anthology of
    Commonwealth Poetry Prize winners.
    1. English poetry — 20th century
    2. English poetry — Commonwealth of
    Nations authors
    I. Niven, Alastair
    821   PR1227

    ISBN 0-85635-729-4

The publishers acknowledge the financial assistance
of the Arts Council of Great Britain and of the
Commonwealth Institute

Typeset in 10pt Palatino by Bryan Williamson, Manchester
Printed in England by SRP Ltd, Exeter

For Isabella and Alexander, two children of the Commonwealth, in the hope that they will grow up to love good poetry and perhaps even to write it.

Contents

Foreword

We are delighted at the publication of this anthology in the Commonwealth Institute's Jubilee Year.

The story of the Prize demonstrates the dramatic changes in the Commonwealth and in the Institute's response to those changes: starting in 1972 with the award of a small prize by a London-based judging panel, selecting only from non-British writers with first collections in English, to a truly Commonwealth-wide group of judges assessing all newly-published poetry in a Commonwealth language for a major international literary award.

This illustrates the consolidation of the Institute as an active proponent of the arts of the Commonwealth which was endorsed by the Heads of Government at their meeting in 1985. Such developments have only been possible as a result of sustained support by the British government, co-operation with Commonwealth governments and enlightened business sponsorship demonstrated so effectively in the case of the Poetry Prize by British Airways.

The Institute believes that by the vigorous presentation of the dynamic work of contemporary artists it is reflecting one of the most persistent and vital elements of the modern Commonwealth. Artists everywhere, and perhaps poets most acutely, address the international dilemmas we face in a way that helps us to understand them better and to appreciate, as Margaret Atwood wrote, that

> . . . surviving
> is the only war
> we can afford.

JAMES PORTER
Director, Commonwealth Institute

Introduction

The Commonwealth Poetry Prize attracts entries from every part of the Commonwealth. It has recognized known and unknown poets and encouraged critical comparisons across continents. The idea of an anthology of winning and commended entries became practicable when enough years had passed to confirm that this Prize was here to stay and had recognized works of sufficient quality to represent Commonwealth poetry as a whole. That point has been reached.

When the Prize was established in 1972 the purse was modest. Poets who were commended received nothing more than a fillip to their reputations. I doubt if the Prize would have survived without the ministrations of the Commonwealth Institute in London, which organizes it and annually plays host to the judges. Michael Foster, the Institute's Librarian, and his colleagues Roger Hughes and Ronald Warwick, were responsible for keeping the Commonwealth Poetry Prize alive in its early years. In 1985, however, British Airways agreed to sponsor both the prize money and the administrative costs. The British Airways Commonwealth Poetry Prize is today a major international award, an enlightened example of the marriage between the arts and business sponsorship. This sponsorship not only ensures over £10,000 of prizes and a better-funded administration; it also means more publicity. An airline is concerned with communication: British Airways' sponsorship of Commonwealth poetry shows that this is interpreted in an imaginative and human way.

Until 1985 there were restrictions on entry to the competition which came to seem absurd to the experts who were annually convened as judges. Among the changes in the regulations that year were four which altered the nature of the Prize. All the poets recognized by the Prize before 1985 were selected by simpler rules: only poets' first books could be submitted. Only poets who wrote in English, and who came from a Commonwealth country other than Britain could enter. The United Kingdom was excluded in the belief that other entries would be swamped by a tidal wave of British poetic brilliance. As a judge on several occasions I found this assumption paternalistic and unjust. Though Britain has the advantage over some Commonwealth countries of a versatile publishing industry, so that more British than other Commonwealth poets are published, there is no monopoly on excellence in Britain. To exclude British poets who address a post-colonial society – as black British and many Scottish, Welsh and regional poets do – seemed unfair.

The Prize excluded until 1985 work not written in English. Changing this rule was more contentious, because "Commonwealth literature" is frequently defined as writing in the English language outside the United States of America. It also poses difficulties for judges who must call on the expertise of those proficient in the proffered alternative languages and rely on translations. But it was an appropriate change, for Commonwealth writers choose their language in very different circumstances: they may come from a monolingual or multi-lingual community, or by their choice of language make an ideological statement, or be part of an indigenous or immigrant minority anxious to preserve its cultural *patrimonie*.

The Prize is no longer reserved for poets' first collections. This has intensified competition and made it more difficult for new writers to gain a footing. But the fourth change to the rules comes in here, for the administration of the Prize was overhauled in 1985, creating categories for winners on a regional basis and an award for the best début. From 1972, when the Commonwealth Poetry Prize began, until 1984 the judges were looking for the best winner from the books submitted. Since then regional winners have been selected from Africa, the Americas, Asia, Australia and the Pacific, and Europe. A "best poet" and a "best first-time published" poet are selected from these regions and forwarded to an international panel which selects the winners in both categories.

In choosing poets for this anthology I decided that it was fairest to include every poet who has won the Prize or been specially commended, and to stop there. Given the space, I would have selected more from any of these writers, and I would have included some of the outstanding entrants over the years whose work was admired though not awarded – Maria Gonzalez from Trinidad for example, whose *Step By Step (Poems 4 to 10)* was published when she was ten years old. But *Under Another Sky* illustrates the diversity of contemporary poetry in the Commonwealth. We have here poems from most of its countries. Occasionally this has given rise to the suspicion that the winners are selected on what the judges called "the Nobel principle" – because it was their country's turn, not because they were the best of the year. No such policy has ever operated.

The poems included here come from different traditions. This has sometimes been a problem for the judges. I hope I am letting

o cats out of the bag if I comment on the two years, 1972 and
979, when the award was shared. The judges in those years
isagreed partly because they were considering poets of out-
tanding quality but also because they themselves were from
ifferent backgrounds which they found hard to reconcile. Some
f them understood the Nigerian literary inheritance of Chinua
chebe and Gabriel Okara, which is rooted in oral poetry and
raws on cultural references unfamiliar to the European reader;
1e other judges admired George McWhirter and Brian Turner
s exponents of a more personal and formally versatile European
adition. Neither group felt at ease with what the other liked,
10ugh the decision to present the award to two poets was amicable
nd recognized the alternative traditions. The organisers of the
rize are aware of this diversity and have always tried to choose
 panel of experts from various backgrounds, but it underlines
1e extent to which the Commonwealth is multi-cultural. Is there
ny point therefore in trying to adjudicate between varying trad-
ions? I believe that there is, first because any international literary
ompetition publicizes writers who might otherwise remain
nknown outside their own country, and also because discussion
f contrasting cultures breaks down the insularity of critics and
aders. A prize that over the years acknowledges poets as different
 themes and styles as Michael Jackson, Arun Kolatkar, David
abydeen and Vikram Seth is not eclectic; it provides evidence
f the range of possibilities in modern English.
  No rules make a writer a Commonwealth writer other than the
ct that he or she is a citizen of a Commonwealth country – and
/en that, as we see in the case of Timothy Holmes, who was
riginally South African but is now Zambian, can be by naturali-
ttion. Indeed, I know no writer from any of the countries rep-
sented here who would call themselves "a Commonwealth poet".
et we can see correspondences between them. Almost all of
1em have something to say about what it means to be a Nigerian
 a New Zealander or from the Caribbean or from India, Australia,
[alaysia, Scotland, or whatever. This may be through comment
1 recent political events, as in Achebe's war poems; but it is
ore likely to be read in their imagery and in a possibly veiled
oint of view. These poets see themselves as helping to forge
2w national traditions independent of the classic lineage of Eng-
h literature, though affected by it. Some of them give primacy
 an inimitable form of English, either rooted in an indigenous
ality or based on a *patois* spoken only in their area. Grace Nichols
1d David Dabydeen are the most obvious examples of this.

13

Others use language more conventionally but bring to their writing a kind of objectivity, even scepticism, that can give them the tone of outsiders looking in on a community to which they do not quite belong. George McWhirter in his Catalan poems, Michael Jackson in his African sequence from which "Return to Lulua-bourg" is taken, Rajagopal Parthasarathy, Timoshenko Aslanides, Shirley Lim, Gary Geddes and Vikram Seth all have this quality, and of course it is there in a different way in Peter Kocan and Robin Thurston, who write from incarceration in an institution. I would claim that it is inherent in the quiet irony and reflective-ness of several of the Antipodean poets in this collection – in Brian Turner, Peter Goldsworthy and Lauris Edmond, for example.

In awarding the Commonwealth Poetry Prize the judges have not been overwhelmed by the multi-national publishers of the western world. They are represented, of course: one admires their determination to publish poetry when it very rarely makes money. It is especially gratifying, however, that smaller publish-ing houses have brought out some of the best poets, and that in the case of Aslanides the work is self-published. There is an inevitable tradition of self-publication in parts of Africa and Asia and among minority groups in multi-cultural societies. The small publisher has to struggle, however, especially in the so-called developing world. I believe it is beyond the comprehension of the average western reader to understand the pressures they are often under, with shortages of ink and paper, a feeble distribution system and the inability of libraries, schools and colleges to acquire the foreign exchange to purchase books. One of the ironies of *Under Another Sky* is that it will be difficult for some of the aspiring writers, students and general readers in the Commonwealth who would most enjoy reading it to do so: they live in areas of the world that are in serious danger of becoming bookless. We hear much about food famines; there are also the famines of the printed word which blight the expectations of many people in the Com-monwealth.

I have taken the title of this book from Parthasarathy's poem "Exile 2", and lest anyone quote the context against me I shall do so myself:

> He had spent his youth whoring
> after English gods.
> There is something to be said for exile:

you learn roots are deep.
That language is a tree, loses colour
under another sky.

Parthasarathy is writing about one of the great issues of Common-wealth writing, the place of English as a language and a cultural resource. All the poets who have won or been commended for the Commonwealth Poetry Prize write in English, either because they have no alternative or because it is the tongue best suited to their intentions. Are they bound to be in thrall to "English gods"? There are those who would say yes – Uganda's late master poet Okot p'Bitek would certainly have done so. This book shows that it need not be so. A poet can use English and be true to a local culture, a private self. In *Under Another Sky* the tree of language flowers, even if it sometimes takes on the appearance of the baobab, which is said to look as though its roots are waving in the wind above the ground.

*

Editor's Notes

Spellings have been retained as they appeared in the original published version of each poem.

In 1975 the Commonwealth Poetry Prize was not awarded, as the judges thought that no entry was of a sufficiently high standard.

Acknowledgements

I would like to express my particular gratitude to Kerry Rankine of the Commonwealth Institute who advised and helped me in the preparation of this anthology and who is a most capable and enthusiastic administrator of the British Airways Commonwealth Poetry Prize. Without her I should have found the task of editing this anthology far harder. I am also very grateful to two of her colleagues, Ronald Warwick and Maggie Butcher, for their assistance and support. Robyn Marsack of Carcanet has been a thoughtful guide to the intricacies of publishing an anthology. Fleur Adcock found me one poet's work when all else had failed. My wife Helen has born the brunt of my late nights when I was making the selection and preparing the text. My thanks to them all.

ALASTAIR NIVEN

CHINUA ACHEBE

Joint Winner 1972 *Beware, Soul Brother*

Chinua Achebe (born 1930) is Nigerian. He is best-known as a novelist: *Things Fall Apart, Arrow of God, No Longer at Ease* and *A Man of the People* have had a profound influence on the development of African literature. After a twenty-one year gap he has returned in 1987 to the novel with *Anthills of the Savannah*. He is also the author of many essays on literature and about contemporary Nigeria. *Beware, Soul Brother* is his only collection of poetry and was published shortly after the end of the Nigerian Civil War.

Beware, Soul Brother

We are the men of soul
men of song we measure out
our joys and agonies
too, our long, long passion week
in paces of the dance. We have
come to know from surfeit of suffering
that even the Cross need not be
a dead end nor total loss
if we should go to it striding
the dirge of the soulful *abia* drums . . .
But beware soul brother
of the lures of ascension day
the day of soporific levitation
on high winds of skysong; beware
for others there will be that day
lying in wait leaden-footed, tone-deaf
passionate only for the deep entrails
of our soil; beware of the day
we head truly skyward leaving
that spoil to the long ravenous tooth
and talon of their hunger.
Our ancestors, soul brother, were wiser
than is often made out. Remember
they gave Ala, great goddess
of their earth, sovereignty too over
their arts for they understood
too well those hard-headed
men of departed dance where a man's
foot must return whatever beauties
it may weave in air, where

17

it must return for safety
and renewal of strength. Take care
then, mother's son, lest you become
a dancer disinherited in mid-dance
hanging a lame foot in air like the hen
in a strange unfamiliar compound. Pray
protect this patrimony to which
you must return when the song
is finished and the dancers disperse;
remember also your children
for they in their time will want
a place for their feet when
they come of age and the dance
of the future is born
for them.

Non-Commitment

Hurrah! to them who do nothing
see nothing feel nothing whose
hearts are fitted with prudence
like a diaphragm across
womb's beckoning doorway to bar
the scandal of seminal rage. I'm
told the owl too wears wisdom
in a ring of defence round
each vulnerable eye securing it fast
against the darts of sight. Long ago
in the Middle East Pontius Pilate
openly washed involvement off his
white hands and became famous. (Of all
the Roman officials before him and after
who else is talked about
every Sunday in the Apostles' Creed?) And
talking of apostles that other fellow
Judas wasn't such a fool
either; though much maligned by
succeeding generations the fact remains
he alone in that motley crowd
had sense enough to tell a doomed

movement when he saw one
and get out quick, a nice little
packet bulging his coat-pocket
into the bargain – sensible fellow.

September, 1970

Christmas in Biafra (1969)

This sunken-eyed moment wobbling
down the rocky steepness on broken
bones slowly fearfully to hideous
concourse of gathering sorrows in the valley
would yet become in another year a lost
Christmas irretrievable in the heights
its exploding inferno transmuted
by cosmic distances to the peacefulness
of a cool twinkling star . . . To death-cells
of that moment came faraway sounds of other
men's carols floating on crackling waves
mocking us. With regret? Hope? Longing? None of
these, strangely, not even despair rather
distilling pure transcendental hate . . .

Beyond the hospital gate
the good nuns had set up a manger
of palms to house a fine plastercast
scene at Bethlehem. The Holy
Family was central, serene, the Child
Jesus plump wise-looking and rose-cheeked; one
of the magi in keeping with legend
a black Othello in sumptuous robes. Other
figures of men and angels stood
at well-appointed distances from
the heart of the divine miracle
and the usual cattle gazed on
in holy wonder . . .

Poorer than the poor worshippers
before her who had paid their homage
of pitiful offering with new aluminium

coins that few traders would take and
a frayed five-shilling note she only
crossed herself and prayed open-eyed. Her
infant son flat like a dead lizard
on her shoulder his arms and legs
cauterized by famine was a miracle
of its own kind. Large sunken eyes
stricken past boredom to a flat
unrecognizing glueyiness moped faraway
motionless across her shoulder . . .

Now her adoration over
she turned him around and pointed
at those pretty figures of God
and angels and men and beasts –
a spectacle to stir the heart
of a child. But all he vouchsafed
was one slow deadpan look of total
unrecognition and he began again
to swivel his enormous head away
to mope as before at his empty distance.
She shrugged her shoulders, crossed
herself again and took him away.

After a War

After a war life catches
desperately at passing
hints of normalcy like
vines entwining a hollow
twig; its famished roots
close on rubble and every
piece of broken glass.

Irritations we used
to curse return to joyous
tables like prodigals home
from the city . . . The metre-man
serving my maiden bill bore
the first friendly face to my circle
of sullen strangers and brought me

smiling gratefully
to the door.

After a war
we clutch at watery
scum pulsating on listless
eddies of our spent
deluge . . . Convalescent
dancers rising too soon
to rejoin their circle dance
our powerless feet intent
as before but no longer
adept contrive only
half-remembered
eccentric steps.

After years
of pressing death
and dizzy last-hour reprieves
we're glad to dump our fears
and our perilous gains together
in one shallow grave and flee
the same rueful way we came
straight home to haunted revelry.

Christmas 1971

GEORGE McWHIRTER

Joint Winner 1972   *Catalan Poems*

George McWhirter (born 1939) is Canadian by adoption, having been born in Belfast, Northern Ireland. Since *Catalan Poems* he has written two poetry cycles, *Queen of the Sea* and *The Island Man*. He is also a short-story writer, his collections including *Bodyworks*, *Counterparts*, and *God's Eye*. *Coming to Grips with Lucy* comprises reminiscences about life in Ireland and British Columbia.

Tarragona Wine

The visitor makes many things of time
in Tarragona: lions in the amphitheatre
that jump to claw from the pit;
seahorses on the sea that lunge at each
other's heels, but fail to bite one moment
back; a cathedral that climbed over
Roman, Gothic, Romanesque –
irreversible.

Senora Valls and Eduardo spend Sunday
there and supervise the time. They trace
the perimeter of the Roman wall. The
wind throws dust in Eduardo's teeth.
Senora Valls walks, protected by a
parasol, her gaze fixed on the wall.

"Think of the amount of time there is in
this wall!" the Senora ponders. Her eyes
widen. They try to encompass time like
the rings of a tree.

"The wall can swallow its tail and stay
around the town forever," Eduardo
attacks her reverie, "but the only time
in Tarragona is in Tarragona wine!"

The Senora's blouse puffs with
unmistakable thunder, but time
inevitably goes on in Tarragona.

Madame

Sensitive like hands,
Eduardo's feet move home
Over warm breasts of concrete,
And the lights wriggle into a girdle,
Split black along the seams.
Tonight,
A sting of cologne in the air,
A smear of red,
Where, behind a haze of windows
The city dresses and waits
To take the world in commerce
With her thighs.

Surreal Appetite

Raura and Dali meet by chance in the
entrance of the market of San José. The
great arc of stained glass above sprays
many-coloured light on their presence.
They agree to accompany each other
and they visit the section of the market
where the animal innards are displayed.
Here, purple hearts with cock-combs of
fat, mauve livers and pale intestines
hang from hooks. Pink lambs' brains
nestle in dishes. In short, every colour
of hoof, head and gut part is exposed.

Dali's moustaches and nostrils quiver.
He proclaims, "When I die, I wish my
long intestine hung here from a golden
hook and my blood made into ruby
puddings. It will be Dali's shrine."

Raura's hands jerk to applaud, but he
notices the queer looks of the stall-
keepers. "Senor Dali, the stall-keepers
here seem a diabolical, shifty-eyed lot.
Once they got your intestine on the
hook, they'd chop it up for American
collectors."

They depart for the fishmarket where Raura watches the lobsters scribble on each other's backs.

"My genitalia have multiplied!" Dali screams. "Look at them on the slab with the small octopus!" A fishwife slaps a kilo of mackerel into a parcel and Raura pulls Dali away. "Oh God, Senor Dali! Look at those fishwives' hands. With one squeeze they shoot eels clean through the ceiling!"

They agree that philistines are a danger to great manifestations and go to a bodega.

"Senor Raura, I propose an immaculate consumption," Dali announces immediately. "A stream of wine at every orifice." And before Raura can add that he would like sardines to accompany, Dali orders.

RICHARD NTIRU

Commended 1972 *Tensions*

Richard Ntiru (born 1946) comes from Kigezi, Uganda and has
written plays and fiction in addition to his poetry. He is a literary
critic, at one time edited the Makarere University newspaper, and
has worked in publishing.

The Prophecy

Who shall console the veiled woman
who buries her head in her wet hands,
who weeps at the folly of weeping
tears that won't dissolve the sour truth
that in a deal between God and man,
God always takes the better bargain?

The cause is as big as a grain of millet.

Who shall console the lonely woman
who sits in a kraal, on this lonely mound,
who sits and sobs,
each sob a knife thrust in her heavy heart,
each tear a drop of blood from her bleeding heart,
each sigh a bubble of life bursting from her lungs?

The cause is as big as a grain of millet.

Who shall feel the sad music
that rides on the waves of her sobs and tears
and rocks her hunched-up form
as she clenches her quivering jaws
gnawing at the eternally elusive truth
that who has known no enemy in his life
idolizes the body?

Who shall share her singular experience
that the cause is as big as a grain of millet?

Why should she sing
when the cause is no more?
Why should she mourn the loss
of what she got beyond expectation?

Why should she resent the equivocal tongue
of the Three Sisters at whose shrine the Oracle said:
>"Daughter of Misfortune
>"A woman is never barren
>"In your last egg, I see a daughter
>"But beware of the bull's horn."

Whose cloudy eye will look back with her,
rocking her baby as she rocks her grief now,
singing to her mirror with maternal glee:
>never go into the sun
>lest you melt away
>never sit in the cold
>lest your blood congeal
>never walk in the dawn
>lest the dew erode your feet
>never walk too far
>lest you stumble and fall
>never come in the bull's way
>lest the prophecy come true

Who shall share the singular experience
that the cause is as big as a grain of millet?

Who shall hear the hunters' cry
the running children's hilarious cry
like leaves singing on the wings of the wind,
the hunting dogs' barks of conquest
like the tribal drums after the war victory;
who shall hear the hunters' cry
that drew the daughter to the gate,
her agemates' ululation
that lured the daughter to the kraal,
the women's circular spinning gyration
that raised the daughter to this lonely mound,
the hunters' spears shimmering with victory
that dazzled the daughter's eyes
and overturned her balance,
thrusting her on the fatal point of the bull's horn
negligently sticking out in the kraal?

Who shall hear the hunters' cry
that brought the prophecy home?

Who shall sit beside this lonely veiled woman
to give a consoling answer to her sodden question:
"Who can prevent the liver of ill luck
from breaking the knife?"

DAVID MITCHELL

Commended 1972   *Pipe Dreams in Ponsonby*

David Mitchell (born 1940) has contributed to many anthologies of New Zealand poetry; *Pipe Dreams in Ponsonby* is his only collection of poems.

Voices

here's yr young married
"happy as th day is long"
spreadeagled on th balcony
of ponsonby
&
tryin t' sing   some song . . .

th post office clock strikes noon
she's read th news
all morning long . . .
she's listened to th radio
(made in hong kong)
she's had coffee with
marlene
(raw sugar / one spoon)
she's discussed th weather
& th fashions & jackie &
th queen . . .
    also th harbour views

now
she's naked on th turkish rug
she bought in anzac avenue
hearing voices drift from th street
like smoke / like dream
& then
  other voices
(she doesn't know whose)

th sun has no history of comfort
that does not become her –
its joy / through th wide windows
of th world
informs her softness

28

with qualities of simple light
from out
        th dark & blue . . .

yet
she sits up suddenly
on scarlet & black
&
taking her head "in her hands"
she weeps
&
at her back/ on th white wall
th girl in th mirror –
th tall
       girl
            weeps
                  too.

WAYNE BROWN

Winner 1973   *On the Coast*

Wayne Brown (born 1944) is a Trinidadian poet who, in addition to his own writing, has edited collections of Caribbean verse. He has also written a biography of the Jamaican sculptress and political figure Edna Manley.

Mackerel

For Tony and Olive McNeill

Deeper, running
Deeper, dropping
Away, slipping
The clutch of our cold sun,
The driven shoal: all but one
Who stayed, turning blandly
About the same calm plaque of sea
On a casual quest, forgetting time.

From the shelf of a rank, barnacled rock
I watched him: vague-tailed, in-
different, almost a drifting crease of blue,
He seemed for a time at ease: secure
With his secret, and indolent with knowledge,
And all given over to the surge of the sea.

                                              Then

Lost, in a quick panic, beating
Left and right, an addict
Scouring his place for some misplaced fix,
Spun by the under-
Waves of time.
                Finally,
Steadied as by a new
Purpose, he sank, fin-thrilling.
His curled blue back shone
Once in a crackle of sunlight and was gone,

And I, staring, peering from my shelf
With the curiosity of a child and a child's
Horror, knew he would not return, though the wild
Cheated gulls churned overhead, screaming.

The green crystal of our nether world
Yielded nothing now; yet
Men will have their truths, their tidy legends,
Their ends: So I

Imagine him, risen elsewhere,
Thrown ashore where the white wave spills
And cooling, his glass eye dulled,
Or crammed to the gills
In the craw of a shark,
Or thrashing, culled,
On the end of a line –

And only deny
That somewhere, hanging in streams
Of light, some ice-blue Purpose
Keeps in quiet its
Unfathomable self,
Given over, all
Over, with easy fins,
To the timeless surge of the sea.

Remu*

1

Cleopatra, washed up nude, sprawled
among the sphinxes. That last bite
and spring-tide of love she chose herself
floated her buttocks and rippled her thighs

Till the remu let her drop and slewed
north, eating Mediterranean.

2

When the oilslicks of the north
crawled south to die on island shores
and remu
went underground. Rose under Peru.

* A tide-race.

31

3

If one day this dull-eyed sea
between the barracks and Gasparee
should boil as at a sharks' feast, know
the remu is passing, mulatto.

4

By love deceived you backed off from
the remu's subterranean whim.
Now your only child is dying, look,
ague shaking him!

5

Maxie drown in de Dragon Mout'.
Fish beating, so he put out.
Greedy make he forget de sun.
Remu take he an' gone.

6

America and Africa
hurled themselves apart,
twin cliffs in the nightsky's blue.
Between them rose the islands,

Between them raced the remu, like panzer-men
through the Ardennes, already in France.

7

I see a child's hand swept among waves
where the remu swings to the open north.
Ah, Mittelholzer!

8

I would write poems like mainsails drawn
up the bent masts of motor schooners
floundering in the remu's flow:
held clear of that chaos but quivering,
holding the strain below.

Fir Tree

for R.D.

At night, distracted, over the town
something goes winging where the old fir tree
keeps its memory still.
It is only the wind, you coolly point,
over our initials, turning leaves.

The book leafs back
to white mornings and the smell of grass,
your swinging plaits, the grinning dog
that ran before us, puppy-bright,
and one other, vaulting in boyhood
over an ominous bar of light.
You clapped and raised it a notch. Ten feet.

Another valley. Another ridge.
Then: "I must be home. Why? Because. Because
it is late. Late."

Oh yes, it was late, the sun said so,
but only your mother cared then.
The clock was lying in wait.

"As this etched tree
endures with our names
we shall endure forever."
                                        And the sun
in the high leaves, dimpling and passing,
the sun in the thicket, gone.

It is late now, passing late, beyond
the time of the sun. The moon crawls
in the roof of our cave.
In the dark
the fir tree is singing to itself.
Its carved heart breaks between us.

Not even your wicked grin can save us now.

On the Coast

". . . words which love had hoped to use,
Erased with the surf's pages."
          Derek Walcott, ISLANDS

I

The light founders. Rain puckers the ocean.
I see a small town, found, then forgotten,
rusting in silence by a sea's edge
where liners no longer come.

You came to me here, bewildered girl,
your body warm and heavy with sleep.
Your eyes were calamitous waters.
How grave were your admonitions!

Later you spoke to me quietly,
as at a distance or under rain
the sea nuzzles her sandspit.
You were beautiful, and I loved you.

Will you never be home again?

II

The warehouse on the waterfront
is empty tonight. The ocean shines.
Moon, it is a winter moon,
a moth's wing netted in cloud.

Why do I sit up these late nights
barefooted on a broken pier?
I never saw galleons enter the moon,
nor the great house that burned on the hill,

And the unpunctual fisherman
who came out of nowhere suddenly
rounding the point on long oars,
had nothing to say to me.

Night, I am getting nowhere.
Island girl, I am scared, don't leave me.

III

Across the bay the streetlamps stare
like amber intersections, and aimlessly
a tree's
shadow splashes the seawall.

The surf turns its pages on dark sand,
the dark boats slip by me as by a lantern,
darkness devours the voices,

And I am an orphaned islander,
on a sandspit of memory,
in a winter
of bays. I have no home.

DENNIS SCOTT

Winner 1974   *Uncle Time*

Dennis Scott (born 1939) is Jamaican and perhaps best known in his own country as a dramatist and theatre director. His plays include *An Echo in the Bone* and *Dog*. Since *Uncle Time* he has written a second collection of poems, *Dreadwalk*.

Exile

There is a kind of loss,
like coming home
to faces; the doors open in-
differently; they whisper,
"Who is this, with dust
in his mouth? Who
is this new traveler?
Tell us of birds,
migrating the dull sky
half a world round,
of Ithaca, and the tiered beast,
of that foreign city
you sent your pale card from!"

There are patterns to assure us:
at table, familiar spices;
the garden, hardly greener;
but something has changed:
clothes we left behind;
the old affections hang loosely.
Suddenly, mouth is dumb; eyes
hurt; surprised, it is we
who have changed; glad, now,
to have practiced loving
before that departure. To travel
is to return
to strangers.

The Compleat Anglers

Trolling for love
without deceit was difficult.
The starfish of our hearts
become dry and sharp
when we take off our bodies, sometimes,
going into the sea.
The sun is unforgiving.

We were at first so
afraid, careful, away from
the safety of flesh; I remember
your questions carved fish
in the nightwall, the sunken gallery
was alive on a sudden with hiding,
finny, hard to catch;
I drew a line
along your mouth, your hand,
and caught doubt.

Now when tides ebb
out to the whisper of deep water
we say true things
or drift in silence, trusting that
away from the incontinent shore
we may come suddenly on
shoals of kindness.

For the Last Time, Fire

That August the birds kept away from the village, afraid:
        people were hungry.
The phoenix hid at the sun's center and stared down
        at the Banker's house,
which was plump and factual, like zero.
Every good Banker knows
there's no such bird.

She came to the house like an old cat, wanting
a different kind of labor.
But the Banker was busy, feeding his dogs, who were nervous,
Perhaps she looked dangerous.
The child threshed in her belly
when she fell. The womb cracked, slack-lipped,
leaving a slight trace of blood on the lawn. Delicately,
the phoenix placed the last straw on its nest.

Mrs So-and-so the Banker's wife beat time
in her withdrawing room. Walked her moods
among the fluted teacups, toying with crusted foods.
The house hummed Bach, arithmetic at rest.
The phoenix sang along with the record,
and sat.
But the villagers counted heads, and got up.

So, logical as that spiral worming the disc to a hole in
                    the center,
one night there were visitors, carrying fire. The dogs
                    died first.
then they gutted everything.

Something shook itself out of the ash.
Wings. Perhaps.

Uncle Time

Uncle Time is a ole, ole man. . . .
All year long 'im wash 'im foot in de sea,
long, lazy years on de wet san'
an' shake de coconut tree dem
quiet-like wid 'im sea-win' laughter,
scraping away de lan' . . .

Uncle Time is a spider-man, cunnin' an' cool,
him tell yu: watch de hill an' yu se mi.
Huhn! Fe yu yi no quick enough fe si
how 'im move like mongoose; man, yu tink 'im fool?

Me Uncle Time smile black as sorrow;
'im voice is sof' as bamboo leaf
but Lawd, me Uncle cruel.
When 'im play in de street
wid yu woman – watch 'im! By tomorrow
she dry as cane-fire, bitter as cassava;
an' when 'im teach yu son, long after
yu walk wid stranger, an' yu bread is grief.
Watch how 'im spin web roun' yu house, an' creep
inside; an' when 'im touch yu, weep. . . .

MICHAEL JACKSON

Winner 1976   *Latitudes of Exile*

Michael Jackson (born 1940) is from New Zealand and since *Latitudes of Exile* he has written two more collections of poems, *Wall* and *Going On*. *Going On* has poems set in France and poems about the death of the poet's wife.

You Learned the Stars

For Bryn

You learned the stars under your
father's hand
and have never lost your way;
even as a boy at sea
without the Southern Cross
in northern latitudes Orion upside down
there was that metal back country road
white in the moonlight, a sea road,
winding down
and the macrocarpa trees
their hands clutching at the sky
in a heavy wind, waves of the sea,
and your father pointing out the stars.

Return from Luluabourg

My report is not of schools
we built out there, or market gardens
planted to help the poor
but of an evening after work
when through a ruined iron gate I saw
a garden overgrown with weeds
and entered it.

Before me rusted boats, swings
dislodged like giants on a dungeon rack,
seesaws split, unpainted, thrown aside,
a wall from which I could not turn my back,
my own hands tied.

That concrete prison drop was set
with broken glass along the top,
bottles once put to European lips
at evening on a patio.
I climbed a metal staircase,
looked across a land scarred red,
huts roofed with grass on which
bone-like manioc roots were dried
to rid them of their arsenic.

But poisons which had touched that place
still kept it out of bounds;
pleasures were gone, children's voices
were not heard
except beyond that wall, in villages
or in the dusk, the garden, one night bird.

To W.H. Auden at 63

When weariness comes with oblique step
over the terrace in late afternoon
and we let slip the murmuring river
and the talk, remembering together
an orchard in our youth . . .
it is then that the intervening shadows
and the single separating pace
are the one hundred thousand deaths,
the vanished faces, the prints they left,
and we, between falling asleep in the sun
and drinking vermouth with a friend
just up from Salzburg, see and hear
the terrible parades of history
dinning into our ears
the barricades of time.

Beyond the overgrown orchard fence
or across the river where willows dip
voices insist that there will always be
such days, yet they grow less
with the light fading, the scraping

of chairs brought in from the colonnade,
and like weariness
the twilight zone scars the earth;
no matter how we judge it now,
it is death.

PETER KOCAN

Commended 1976   *The Other Side of the Fence*

Peter Kocan (born 1947) comes from New South Wales, Australia. Much of his poetry is about life in institutions for people with psychological disorders. He has written another collection of poems called *Armistice* (1978).

The Hospital Kangaroos

They are the real spirits of the place,
Having endured a million years
Of bush-silence and bush-darkness.

We see them at morning and afternoon
Browsing through meadowland
At roadside, or brooding beneath trees

Motionless as their own images
Daubed in ochre upon the rock walls
Of pre-history.

In their eyes the apathy
Of a played-out breed, broken
By the monotony of survival.

In their gestures a caution
Sprung less from fear
Than primordial habit. They dwell at the fringe

Of our lives, tolerated
For cuteness or curiosity, prey
To camera and larrikin's gun.

They are the real spirits of the place,
Waiting mutely, year to year,
Like sufferers who perceive an end.

ROBIN THURSTON

Commended 1976   *Believed Dangerous*

Robin Thurston (born 1945), who comes from New Zealand, at the time of publishing *Believed Dangerous* had served several years as a prisoner for bank-robbing crimes. He has described each poem he writes as 'an act of bravado'.

Female Prisoners – Boggo Road

(Watched from the showerblock – which I clean)
     mad as magpies, they squat about the yard
     knees splayed (no man to close them for)
     and innocent, chortling over marbles
     snatched up with screeching ribaldry.

     But soon, herded by shadows, they'll sit
     in the corner like maids, slump laphanded
     and ruined (that by rape, or ripping birth
     unpaints such faces) – accepting – bonded
     in that female way, in crisis or pity

     to wait for tea or kindness. Up here
     (Footsteps on the walk) the Giant stirs
     in his sleep, and I, no Jack, descend.
     But yet – am seen!   Waving,
     she shows me her breast and laughs.

     I lie awake, recapturing.

ARUN KOLATKAR

Winner 1977   *Jejuri*

Arun Kolatkar (born 1932) comes from Kolhapur in India and writes in both English and Marathi, sometimes translating between the two languages. He is also a well-known graphic artist. The poems in *Jejuri* collectively portray the life of a small Indian community.

Heart of Ruin

The roof comes down on Maruti's head.
Nobody seems to mind.

Least of all Maruti himself.
May be he likes a temple better this way.

A mongrel bitch has found a place
for herself and her puppies

in the heart of the ruin.
May be she likes a temple better this way.

The bitch looks out at you guardedly
past a doorway cluttered with broken tiles.

The pariah puppies tumble over her.
May be they like a temple better this way.

The black eared puppy has gone a little too far.
A tile clicks under its foot.

It's enough to strike terror in the heart
of a dung beetle

and send him running for cover
to the safety of the broken collection box

that never did get a chance to get out
from under the crushing weight of the roof beam.

No more a place of worship this place
is nothing less than the house of god.

Between Jejuri and the Railway Station

You leave the little temple town
with its sixty three priests inside their sixty three houses
huddled at the foot of the hill
with its three hundred pillars, five hundred steps and eighteen arches.
You pass the sixty fourth house of the temple dancer
who owes her prosperity to another skill.
A skill the priest's son would rather not talk about.
A house he has never stepped inside
and hopes he never will.
You pass by the ruin of the temple but the resident bitch is nowhere around
You pass by the Gorakshanath Hair Cutting Saloon.
You pass by the Mhalasakant Cafe
and the flour mill.
And that's it.
The end.
You've left the town behind
with a coconut in your hand,
a priest's visiting card in your pocket
and a few questions knocking about in your head.
You stop halfway between
Jejuri on the one and the railway station on the other hand.
You stop dead
and stand still like a needle in a trance.
Like a needle that has struck a perfect balance between equal scales
with nothing left to add or shed.

What has stopped you in your tracks
and taken your breath away
is the sight
of a dozen cocks and hens in a field of jowar
in a kind of a harvest dance. The craziest you've ever seen.
Where seven jump straight up to at least four times their height
as five come down with grain in their beaks.

up   aⁿd   do_wn   a_nd   u p   &   d

   &   d   a   p^u   a_nd do_w & u p

wo_n   n   n

n   u_p   an d o w_n &   u an d d o n a_nd u_p

     d   p

o & u aⁿ d   d_ow_n a_nd u ^p a_dn _down_&&_&

w   p

n_d u^p a u^p a_nd d^woⁿ a n d a_dn u^p

     d n

And there you stand forgetting how silly you must look
with a priest on your left shoulder as it were
and a station master on your right.

The Station Master

the booking clerk believes in the doctrine
of the next train
when conversation turns to time
he takes his tongue
hands it to you across the counter
and directs you to a superior
intelligence

the two headed station master
belongs to a sect
that rejects every timetable
not published in the year the track was
laid as apocryphal
but interprets the first timetable
with a freedom that allows him to read
every subsequent timetable between
the lines of its text

RAJAGOPAL PARTHASARATHY

Commended 1977   *Rough Passage*

Rajagopal Parthasarathy (born 1934) comes from India and has a
Tamil background. He has been writing poetry since the 1960s.
Rough Passage is a three-part poem, examining the problems of
language and identity when one feels oneself both to be part of a
diverse Indian culture and greatly influenced by the west.

Exile: 2

Through holes in a wall, as it were,
lamps burned in the fog.
In a basement flat, conversation

filled the night, while Ravi Shankar,
cigarette stubs, empty bottles of stout
and crisps provided the necessary pauses.

He had spent his youth whoring
after English gods.
There is something to be said for exile:

you learn roots are deep.
That language is a tree, loses colour
under another sky.

The bark disappears with the snow,
and branches become hoarse.
However, the most reassuring thing

about the past is that it happened.
Dressed in tweeds or grey flannel,
its suburban pockets

bursting with immigrants –
"coloureds" is what they call us
over there – the city is no jewel, either:

lanes full of smoke and litter,
with puddles of unwashed
English children.

On New Year's Eve he heard an old man
at Trafalgar Square: "It's no use trying
to change people. They'll be what they are.

An empire's last words are heard
on the hot sands of Africa.
The da Gamas, Clives, Dupleixs are back.

Victoria sleeps on her island
alone, an old hag,
shaking her invincible locks."

Standing on Westminster Bridge,
it seemed the Thames had clogged
the chariot wheels of Boadicea to a stone.

Under the shadow of poplars
the river divides the city from the night.
The noises reappear,

of early trains, the milkman,
and the events of the day become
vocal in the newsboy.

TIMOSHENKO ASLANIDES

Winner 1978   *The Greek Connection*

Timoshenko Aslanides (born 1943) is the son of a Greek father and an Australian mother and is himself part of the large "Greek connection" which helps to make Australia a multi-cultural society. His poetry includes a collection entitled *One Hundred Riddles*.

Imitation of Intimations

I? Take immortality? Were it offered,
I'd refuse – I have it! No need for double
measure. Listen how, without any trouble,
      seven rhymed Sapphics

(Taken from the land of my father) just pour
out, across the page, spreading trochees and spond-
ees around, like drunks at a bistro so fond,
      now, of the house red

That they ramble 'round, in a noisy congress,
T-boned and tiddly, while each one of them thinks
he (or she) is there for some reason: drinks, winks,
      – kinks? Yet not knowing

That, together they have some higher purpose:
Bacchic rites, now suitably modernized. Well,
similarly (wow!) the few words I can spell
      push for the prime parts

In my poem, elbowing for   position,
pushing aside syntax and punctuation
for the mythological titbits fashion
      needs for show: "How did

Diomedes do it? And what songs did those
Sirens sing?" I shout: enough!! Let's forget what
Diomedes did. Or how Thracian whores got
      Orpheus by the

Short and curlies. Just what is happening now?
Why is my glass empty? Look sharp there. Fill me
up with that red wine. How else can my skill be
      heard, if I'm not drunk?

Prayer to Aphrodite

Why now tempt me? Why do you do this? OK
so she's pretty. Beautiful even. But. Why
put her near me. Here, on this empty bus? You
      knew that I'd want her,

Didn't you? Yet, you were aware that I'm still
shy. You raised me. Timid, and prudish. Damn it!
Sydney. 1960. And still I dread my
      wanting a woman.

Look! Her eye! Once. Twice. And she clearly wants you.
Turn to her. Speak. Ask her the time of day. Say
something! Tongue tied terror won't win a woman.
      You have to speak first.

What to say, though? Time and the weather are out.
Two more people boarded the bus then. Do you
want me looking mad, a prize nitwit? See. They
      sit right behind us.

Can't I maintain even the pretence? Reading
lines that I know can't help me breathe one
single word? Now, looking back, four eyes say: go,
      move across. Pressure

Mounts. My book sweats. Both of us fear a put-down.
If I don't ask, how will I ever know her?
Love her? This girl: black-haired and sun-brown, full-lipped;
      give me some help, words;

Let me speak. You know you've the power. I can't
do it myself. Better still, let her utter
some remark. I'm done. If she says get lost, four
      souls see me suffer.

The Island of the Sirens

I, Ulysses, refuse to learn the songs
the Sirens sing – though all around me throngs
of sailors who have learnt them say to me:

Listen! Sing them! The heady harmonies
will blow your mind. Forget the unknown seas,
they say, and settle for these sound, established

Tunes. The melodies are easy – no need
to know notation. Just sing along! Indeed!
I've heard! I took their distant rhymes to be

Quite attractive. Compelling even. But how
long do you think I'd last, singing from the bow
with someone else's song? Start, and you're finished.

KEVIN HART

Commended 1978   *The Departure*

Kevin Hart (born 1954) emigrated from England, where he lived
until the age of twelve, to Brisbane, Australia. He is the author of
a second collection, *The Lines of the Hand: Poems 1976-79*. Charles
Conder (1868-1909) was an English painter who worked for a time
in Australia.

The Departure

(Charles Conder)

First and last – the people, dressed up and down
in black along the quay, beneath umbrellas
raised in dull acclaim at another loss
as the boat heaves out of dock. Some frown
at others who turn away, aware of rain
collapsing above their heads, and casually
forget the son or husband they cannot see
hauling his gear beneath the deck. The lane
crawls off, bloated with bodies, as each now makes
his way back home to what a home can give.
Smoke stains the sky from ferries undoing the water
behind them. It's morning: the sea tosses and wakes,
groping for colour it has lost; men now live
aboard, silently watching loved faces blur.

GABRIEL OKARA

Joint Winner 1979   *The Fisherman's Invocation*

Gabriel Okara (born 1921) was a well-known Nigerian poet long
before his success in the Commonwealth Poetry Prize, though *The
Fisherman's Invocation* was his first full-length collection. He is the
author of a much discussed novel, *The Voice*, in which he experi-
ments with a form of English heavily influenced by the Ijaw language
of his area of eastern Nigeria. Much of his writing was in manu-
script form only when it was lost in the Nigerian Civil War.

The Snowflakes Sail Gently Down

The snowflakes sail gently
down from the misty eye of the sky
and fall lightly on the
winter-weary elms. And the branches
winter-stripped and nude, slowly
with the weight of the weightless snow
bow like grief-stricken mourners
as white funeral cloth is slowly
unrolled over deathless earth.
And dead sleep stealthily from the
heater rose and closed my eyes with
the touch of silk cotton on water falling.

Then I dreamed a dream
in my dead sleep. But I dreamed
not of earth dying and elms a vigil
keeping. I dreamed of birds, black
birds flying in my inside, nesting
and hatching on oil palms bearing suns
for fruits and with roots denting the
uprooters' spades. And I dreamed the
uprooters tired and limp, leaning on my roots –
their abandoned roots
and the oil palms gave them each a sun.

But on their palms
they balanced the blinding orbs
and frowned with schisms on their
brows – for the suns reached not
the brightness of gold!

54

Then I awoke. I awoke
to the silently falling snow
and bent-backed elms bowing and
swaying to the winter wind like
white-robed Muslims salaaming at evening
prayer, and the earth lying inscrutable
like the face of a god in a shrine.

One Night at Victoria Beach

The wind comes rushing from the sea,
the waves curling like mambas strike
the sands and recoiling hiss in rage
washing the Aladuras'* feet pressing hard
on the sand and with eyes fixed hard
on what only hearts can see, they shouting
pray, the Aladuras pray; and coming
from booths behind, compelling highlife
forces ears; and car lights startle pairs
arm in arm passing washer-words back
and forth like haggling sellers and buyers –

Still they pray, the Aladuras pray
with hands pressed against their hearts
and their white robes pressed against
their bodies by the wind; and drinking
palmwine and beer, the people boast
at bars at the beach. Still they pray.

They pray, the Aladuras pray
to what only hearts can see while dead
fishermen long dead with bones rolling
nibbled clean by nibbling fishes, follow
four dead cowries shining like stars
into deep sea where fishes sit in judgement;
and living fishermen in dark huts
sit round dim lights with Babalawo
throwing their souls in four cowries
on sand, trying to see tomorrow.

* *Aladuras: a Christian sect addicted to ritual bathing*

Still, they pray the Aladuras pray
to what only hearts can see behind
the curling waves and the sea, the stars
and the subduing unanimity of the sky
and their white bones beneath the sand.

And standing dead on dead sands,
I felt my knees touch living sands –
but the rushing wind killed the budding words.

Dispensing Morning Balm

Dispensing morning balm
in crystal drops of songs
into the yawning city
and the rumble and asthmatic
whizzing of a young day,
these birds erase dreams
and nightmares of the fading darkness.

BRIAN TURNER

Joint Winner 1979   *Ladders of Rain*

Brian Turner (born 1944) comes from Dunedin, New Zealand. His collections of poetry, in addition to *Ladders of Rain*, include *Ancestors, Listening to the River* and *Bones*. He is a free-lance writer, and now edits the poetry list of the publisher John McIndoe.

Hawk

The hawk is alone
in the ownerless sky.
He glides over fields
and soars above the hills:
believe me, he will sell

his supremacy dear. The
casual ease of his flight
deceives the uninitiated:
that haughty, languidly
sweeping hook-nosed bird

spells threat, death. He
is prying Director,
is the smarmy Al Capone
of the air; the shushing wing-beat
harbours the sound

of cruising limousines. All
that tremble tremble with just
fear for he does not
intend to stay long
up there alone in the air . . .

No hawk is real hawk
without hot blood
besmirching his beak, without
flesh gripped between the sharp
God-given claws of his feet.

For an Octogenarian

Whistling like a goat pissing on a tin lid
remote and not caring to be reached
but not yet out in the cold.
Resting, propped in the sun,
small and frail sliver of a man
full of kindness and unconcerned with guilt;
my mother says you were lazy
but you never seemed to care.
      Well, what do you hear,
what do you listen for, to, sitting there
in the barely-warm July sun,
on a raft of glittering light, Flagstaff
hunched in a shoddy snow-flecked winter coat,
the surf dinning beyond the dunes
100 yards from your back door?
      Your body renders thin shadows,
reedy nuances of night and day,
of men puzzled by more than the dazzle
of direct, nervy sunlight,
abraded and clammy with cowardice
and sham and unconcern:
      how convenient
the lame consciences that fade as quickly
as radios turned down.
      What do we know of living together,
of dreams that soar and tug like bright kites
in the light of the setting sun,
of the lick of the wind, the languid banalities of summer?
      Man whom I knew I never knew,
I shall remember you as a too human face
peeping from a trench in a feather mattress,
the touch of a hand in the manacling dark,
the first and last grandfather I will never know.

Watch for the Ice

for Jo Hansen

Here one day, gone the next:
nothing unusual in that. The earth
caught in the grip of winter,

wet hibernation. But very much alive,
as we are alive and the blood
quickens when clouds blow over

and the sun shines on bare trees
and frosty grass . . . unashamed
celebration of the pastoral,

embodying a wish to live unwished
and without concern for rewards.
Ah, if it were that simple.

We forget what we want to
remember: the demons batter the glass.
Watch for the ice; watch for the ice

as you go, speculative, loosening, essential . . .

SHIRLEY LIM

Winner 1980   *Crossing the Peninsula and Other Poems*

Shirley Geok-lin Lim (born 1944) was the first woman and the first Malaysian to win the Commonwealth Poetry Prize. She comes from Malacca but now lives in the United States of America. A more recent collection of poems is *No Man's Grove*, published in Singapore.

Modern Secrets

Last night I dreamt in Chinese.
Eating Yankee shredded wheat
I said it in English
To a friend who answered
In monosyllables:
All of which I understood.

The dream shrank to its fiction.
I had understood its end
Many years ago. The sallow child
Ate rice from its ricebowl
And hides still in the cupboard
With the china and tea-leaves.

Women's Dreams

Women spin dreams all hours of the day;
At night the naked light spits its light
On our hairy parts. The gay says,
You women do not know how to love.
Yes, wilfully we choose the ill-matched mate,
Delight in the effort to fit.
Being Mother Nature and our own creation.
Puzzles, tricks, stratagems: we match wits
Because we have not known dominion.
Initiates balance breast and buttock,
Colour faces, depilate their arm-pits;
But, desperadoes on the run, they hatch

Bat-like in the furred, mammalian cave.
Women are crones still, clumsy magicians.
Even fat and ugly may stir a cock
And lord it for a day and a night.

Monsoon History

The air is wet, soaks
Into mattresses, and curls
In apparitions of smoke.
Like fat white slugs furled
Among the timber,
Or silver fish tunnelling
The damp linen covers
Of schoolbooks, or walking
Quietly like centipedes,
The air walking everywhere
On its hundred feet
Is filled with the glare
Of tropical water.

Again we are taken over
By clouds and rolling darkness.
Small snails appear
Clashing their timid horns
Among the morning glory
Vines.
            Drinking milo,
Nonya and baba sit at home.
This was forty years ago.
Sarong-wrapped they counted
Silver paper for the dead.
Portraits of grandfathers
Hung always in the parlour.

Reading Tennyson, at six
p.m. in pyjamas,
Listening to down-pour-
ing rain: the air ticks
With gnats, black spiders fly,
Moths sweep out of our rooms

Where termites built
Their hills of eggs and queens zoom
In heat. We wash our feet
For bed, watch mother uncoil
Her snake hair, unbuckle
The silver mesh around her waist,
Waiting for fathers pacing
The sand as fishers pull
From the Straits after monsoon.

The air is still, silent
Like sleepers rocked in the pantun,
Sheltered by Malacca.
This was forty years ago,
When nyonya married baba.

AUDREY LONGBOTTOM

Commended 1980   *Relatives and Reliques*

Audrey Longbottom comes from New South Wales, Australia, and has published poems and stories in many Australian journals. Since *Relatives and Reliques* she has written more poems, collected in *The Solitary Islands*.

Resolution

Tomorrow
will be
different
I'll get up early
organise the children
send them neatly to school
my husband quietly to work
and I shall surprise
with gentleness eyes
lowered
dressed in blue
smelling of lavender
hair parted in the
middle

SHOUTING IS OVER AND
the little monsters gone
hot-eyed to school after
placating the cat kicked only
beyond its dignity and him at
work no doubt extracting the barbs
of insults well earned and aimed
now I shall clear away the muck of this
half eaten breakfast then get dressed
and by tonight it will be all right and
Tomorrow
will be
different

63

PHILIP SALOM

Winner 1981 *The Silent Piano*

lip Salom (born 1950) was born on a dairy farm in Western Australi
followed up *The Silent Piano* with a poetry sequence entitled *T
jectionist*. Salom illustrates his poems with his own woodcuts.

Bushfire

I

As if going into battle, the knapsack
full on my shoulders, its pipe and nozzle
slung up like a rifle.
We fought along the river, seeing shrubs
explode, riddled with fire,
eerie sounds of trees shrieking
like things alive, feral, flames like faces
spilling down into the ferns.
We staggered, sick with the hammering heat,
dousing endless flames that slammed at us
like nightmares, sullen ghosts
groping at our limbs. We plunged
into that day's red thunder,
subsumed like suiciders who stare into
the rifle, gulp the flame. Individuals
meandering in something huge.
We choked through the lead-coloured
air of limbo.

Now the aching blistering weight
of the knapsack pulling my shoulders.
Exhaustion worries the scorched end
of some unity: thought and action
fused into one. Sagging now,
heavier than the slopping drums
behind the tractors coming in.
We see the new men walking in
and seem to meet our earlier selves
but are more certain and more tired.
I, older than my youth, seeing these men
as if they were children.

II

From an unseen movement
of pores and sticks,
insects stitch the heat.
Dragon-flies hover above the dam,
their wings rustle and blur.
Empty chrysalis shine,
translucent, on reeds.
The brown water sinks.

I swear at the dogs
sneaking into the shade or slipping
beneath fences to hang
their tongues in the dam.

See now the dairy's iron roof
ebbing and distorting in the haze,
as cows file along the race.
And I see through different heat
black stumps in lines, iron-rimmed
tractors, rusting now to pretend
this red identity of fire after
the flame. Or the bent girders, claws,
roof-iron punched into curves
by the pugilist fire.

Blackened cattle, like flawed statues
for a day, crammed into fence corners
where they tore at life
as death mounted them and sang
from a wobbling, distorted mouth.

III

The noise of heat. Strange pressure on my eardrums
sound on so many unseen nerves.
Bush like a shaman's spittle,
sand, powder and breath, crash
of an animal leaping in the bracken:
spirits in the gritty palm. Murmurings,
as if soil or rabbits' fur sensed
stoma gossiping of saps' events,

or snakes in the undergrowth,
or wedge-tails stirring the tree-tops
seized in a day's talon.
Heat and sound, like a mind knowing
the bushes' circle: wood, carcasses,
fragments in the mesh of ants,
eaten down to sand. Around,
around. Green buds
humming on the spindle of black trees.
Suddenly coming upon the shape:
black, molten body of a kangaroo
sagging to the ground, its feet
caught in the fence's top barb
that snatched in flight, fire shrieking all around,
flames that raced on flesh,
like a conductor – to the ground.

Cattle Sale

I lay, rumpled like a lizard in the sun,
on the wide top-rail, the split wood pressing
against my back, the sale dragging on;
saw something in the sky, bodied, juggled
by flight: then, clearly, it was Icarus
gold skinned through unfathered air, wings
fluted in brilliance along his spine,
in sheer flight conceived by virgins,
hauled in fantasy towards the sun.
Became aware again, through the levelling
air, plunged.

PETER GOLDSWORTHY

Winner 1982   *Readings from Ecclesiastes*

Peter Goldsworthy (born 1951) comes from South Australia where today he is a general practitioner in medicine. His sharp and often ironic poetry is matched by his short stories, some of which are collected in a book called *Archipelagoes*.

Ecclesiastes

(After Kampuchea)

Give me no more lessons of history.
No more fatherlands or economics.
Enough words.

My head is choked with their gristle.
With too many lies. With words
that kill children who have no words.

A scream was the first word,
and will be the last. The grammar of pain
dissolving under tongues of earth.

If at all, let language be better than this.
As pure as the verbs of algebra,
or the distance of tongues.

Or louder than words –
burning books, attacking trees,
consuming the air that cruelly allows speech.

Like defeated kings
putting oceans to the sword –
one more lesson of history.

A Shoeshine for Louis Armstrong

How perfectly
the gramophone remembers

your trumpet's sweet blasphemy
the blackness of your voice.

A voice as black
as I am green,

my words will never have this ease
this happiness of lips on brass

or fingers slipping on chords
like cool ivory gloves.

The air is slippery with jazz
with perfectly remembered blues,

and all that words can do
is shine shine your shoes.

Act Six

Act six begins
when the curtain falls,
the corpses awake,
the daggers are cleaned.

Act six
is Juliet in the supermarket,
Mr Macbeth on the 8.15.

In act six
Hamlet sucks a tranquilliser,
Romeo washes up

and death
is gentle and anonymous –
Lear's respirator
switched discreetly off.

Arson

I burn your letters
at the edge of night
– an autumn bonfire.

Into the flames
go leaves fallen from trees,
and those brought in the post.

Garden prunings,
and the foliage of desks
– drafts of unfinished pain.

Slowly the flames contract
to a fistful of ashes,
a finger of smoke in the night.

Even the stars we see
are only a kind of memory,
already dead for years.

GRACE NICHOLS

Winner 1983   *I is a long memoried woman*

Grace Nichols (born 1950) is Guyanese but has been living in England since the late 1970s where she has become one of the most popular feminist poets. Her second collection, *The Fat Black Woman's Poems*, wittily reverses some of the stereotypes of black womanhood. Her novel of Guyanese life at the time of her own childhood, *Whole of a Morning Sky*, has the same accurate ear as her poetry for local nuances of language.

We the Women

We the women who toil
unadorn
heads tie with cheap
cotton

We the women who cut
clear fetch dig sing

We the women making
something from this
ache-and-pain-a-me
back-o-hardness

Yet we the women
who praises go unsung
who voices go unheard
who deaths they sweep
aside
as easy as dead leaves

I Will Enter

Singed by a flight of scarlet ibises
blinded like a grasshopper by the rains

tattered and hungry
you took me in

gave me cassava bread
and casirri

a hammock to sleep in

a blanket woven by
your own hands
rich with embroidery

I will enter   into you
I will enter   into you
               woman

through the Indian forest
of your hair
I will enter

through the passage of your
wary watchful eyes
I will enter

through the bitterness
of your cassava touch
I will enter

And when you are moonsick
I will bleed with you

But wait
like a broken flute
your tongue is silent
your eyes speak of an
ancient weariness
I too have known
memory is written
in each crumpled fold
you can still remember
how they pitted gun against
arrow
steel against stillness

Stunned by their demands
for gold

And so you'll talk no more
of Amalivaca
or the mystery of his strange
rock writings

No more of Kaie
brave old chief who took
to sacrifice on behalf
of his tribe
rushing the falls before
the great Mokonima's eye

Eulogy

Everywhere I hear them whispering
in ruptured tones of nostalgia
voices pushed in by the sea breeze
darting like pains in my heads

cadences like the living
    parables of the dead

Yes the souls
Yes the souls
Yes the souls
caught in the Middle Passage
limbo

the dead ones
who are not dead
the sleeping ones
who are not sleeping

the restless ones
the leaping suicide
ones . . . . . . the saddest
ones of all who toss and
moan
with each lash of the ocean
foam

Everywhere I hear them whispering
in ruptured tones of nostalgia
voices pushed in by the sea breeze
darting like pains in my head

cadences like the living
parables of the dead

Yes the souls
Yes the souls
Yes the souls
caught in the Middle Passage
limbo

How can I eulogise
their names?
What dance of mourning
can I make?

How can I eulogise
their names?
What dance of mourning
can I make?

Dayadu, Ishiodu, Anamadi
plunging wildly to the waters
of your fate
Kobidja, Nwasobi, Okolie
swallowing your own tongues
cold and stiff on your chains

How can I eulogise your names
What dance of mourning can I make?

GEOFFREY URSELL

Commended 1983   *Trap Lines*

Geoffrey Ursell (born 1943) has written mainly about his own are
Canada, which is Saskatchewan. In addition to *Trap Lines*, a collec
concerned with the animal and human life of remote areas in Can
he has written several plays, among them *The Running of the Deer*
Saskatoon Pie!.

Beaver Love

as the beaver
loves the Willow

so do you love me

you eat the bark
destroy the tree

DAVID DABYDEEN

Winner 1984   *Slave Song*

avid Dabydeen (born 1955) was brought up in Guyana but moved
England when he was fourteen. He is now an academic and
s publications include a book on the portrayal of black people
the paintings of William Hogarth. David Dabydeen is also an
ticulate spokesperson for black aspirations in Britain. In the *Slave*
ng sequence of poems he creates a form of creolized English
milar to that used by the plantation slaves in the Caribbean.

Slave Song

e me haan up.
k out me eye.
aal me teet out
me na go bite.
ut chain rung me neck.
ish me foot tight.
t yu daag fo gyaad
aan till nite –

u yu caan stap me cack floodin in de goldmine
aan stap me cack splashin in de sunshine!

hip me till me bleed
ll me beg.
ll me how me hanimal
frican orang-utan
ll me how me cannibal
t fo slata fit fo hang.
ice waan lip out
aan ear an waan leg –

u yu caan stap me cack dippin in de honeypot
ippin at de tip an happy as a hottentot!

ok how e'ya leap from bush to bush like a black crappau
eking out a watahole,
ind by de sunflare, tongue like a dussbowl –
e how e'ya sip laang an full an slow!

ll e swell an heavy, stubban, chupit, full o sleep
ke camoudie swalla calf an stretch out in de grass, content,

75

Full o peace . . .
Hibiscus bloom, a cool breeze blow
An from a hill a wataflow
Canary singin saaf an low . . .

Is so when yu dun dream she pink tit,
Totempole she puss,
Leff yu teetmark like a tattoo in she troat!

She gi me taat
She gi me wife
So tear out me liver
Or stake me haat
Me still gat life!

Two Cultures

"Hear how a baai a taak
Like BBC!
Look how a baai a waak
Like white maan,
Caak – hat pun he head, wrist – watch pun he haan!
Yu dadee na Dabydeen, plant gyaden near Blackbush Pass
He na cut wid sickle an dig wid faak?
He na sell maaket, plantain an caan?
An a who pickni yu rass?
Well me never see story like dis since me baan!

E bin Inglan two maaning, illegal,
Eye-up waan-two white hooman,
Bu is wha dem sweet watalily seed
Go want do wid hungrybelly Blackbush weed
Like yu, how yu teet yella like dhall
An yu tongue black like casrip!
Dem should a spit, vamit pun yu, beat yu rass wid whip
Is lungara like yu spoil dem good white people country,
Choke an rab, bruk-an-enta, tief dem people prapaty!

So yu tink yu can come hey an play big-shat,
Fill we eye wid cigarette, iceapple an all dat?
Aweh po country people bu aweh ga pride:
Jess touch my gyal-pickni, me go buss yu back-side."

76

LAURIS EDMOND

Winner 1985   *Selected Poems*

Lauris Edmond (born 1924) is from New Zealand. Her first collec-
tion, *In Middle Air* did not appear until 1975. *Selected Poems* contains
work from all her main collections: *In Middle Air, The Pear Tree,
Wellington Letter, Salt from the North* and *Catching It*. Another vol-
ume, *Seasons and Creatures*, was published in 1986. She has the
distinction of being the first overall winner of the British Airways
Commonwealth Poetry Prize under the wider terms that were
introduced in 1985.

Femme Agée

I was pretty once, I say it judiciously,
and he was mad for me, but I married my one
true love, my laughing companion; the other – he
went into the church. Now both are dead. Alone
I have to be the creature I've become –
the cruel jailer that was born in me and, since
it will not want to die, now takes my form.
I am disgusting to myself who once
was beautiful to them: that trembling jaw,
my clumsy step supported by a stick,
the veined old hand that grips it like a claw
– no man could so possess me, nor so mock.
Was this the pact my faithless body made?
Only a woman can be so betrayed.

The Study of Geography, or History

and a gesture of opposition to George Steiner

At school I scribbled in the margin of my atlas –
not liking facts connected with production, weather,
population, soil, I chose instead to wander
in countries never mentioned: Babylon, Byzantium,
the Persian city still called Tyre, or Samarkand
(and peacocks strutting in courtyards of milk-white marble),
    Carthage,
golden city buried deeper than the tombs of Pharaohs;
even Abyssinia where, I had been told,

men sliced their meat off rumps of rams still running
wild – the screams of those terrified creatures were louder
than any teacher's exhortations to "attend".

Tonight in a small white house, in the raw country I
have always lived in, I listen to a cultivated
European voice say in English that
men are guests upon the earth: "man is a cruel
carnivore built to move forward . . . but the truth
may be extraneous to his needs . . ." The truth? So used
it is a scientists' word. Once more I see the sun god,
god of death, the falcon and the jackal, brooding
over the Old Kingdom, and Doric tribes building
temples of stone when Pompeii was a country town.
Above me the starlit southern sky shines with a patient
attentive brilliance on the dreams of hopeful men.

The truth – what is it but the answer men in time may give
to questions asked by men? If the future of a dying
universe is told in gaseous explosions
amid uninhabitable rocks, then
here, in the silence of a summer night where
the small cottages lie asleep, and the strangely
transparent faces of the moon flowers are lit up in the garden,
I affirm my tenuous humanity. The lost
territories of Byzantium, this village here – these
hold all the future I can recognise; I am afraid
of a star spinning into darkness unseen by living
eyes; or the truth that knows no voice to say its name.

Greek Antiquities: First Floor

Little sculptured animals, young deer
still stiffly running, still with bright
and frightened eyes, my fingers touch
the tiny perforations that mark
the spots upon your coats of clay
and find them rough and hard. Will any
dream of mine so run, wakeful
through more than twenty centuries?

Morning in Christchurch

Through the singing of birds I rise
slowly from sleep; this garden, the city,
these islands have moved into morning;
over the sea that wraps the unreachable
curves of the earth, continents sleep.
It is dark in New York. Last night I read
that Robert Lowell is dead – and look
now towards that populous American night
wondering, puzzling . . . for it is not grief
we feel at a great man's death, but a kind
of apprehension, as though some piece
of a vivid pattern has dropped
from its place, and left a darkness
we know to be ours. I imagine the rooms,
the desks under lamps, the rough tables
where men and women will search with
judicious patience for a new light,
remembering the place where he gathered
his graveyards and grainy seas, his rooms
full of angular eccentric relations
and tortured heroes; his grim wisdom.

TIMOTHY HOLMES

Best first-time published poet 1985   *Double Element*

Timothy Holmes (born 1936) was originally South African and grew up in Natal. He has lived in Zambia since 1963 and is now a citizen of that country. Though *Double Element* was a first book, Timothy Holmes's poems were included many years before in an influential anthology entitled *Seven South African Poets*.

Melodious Birds

Your immediate worry is over;
The rough hike through the valley
And foot by foot clamber
Up a vertiginous escarpment
Have yielded you an undulating plain
Replete with small lake, gentle
Trees, an ice-clear stream, rushes,
Melodious birds; a place to rest.

Dip your hot feet in water; cast
An eye back over all the gentlefolk
Who, battles over, empires lost or won,
Have settled to write their days
Away by watersides:
                    But don't ask the question
We could put their ghosts:
A dove absorbed on buzzard's eggs
Sits comfortably upon its breezy nest.

Snow Fell

A leopard came to drink:
Fleet leopard with a spot
Upon the heart. To the hollowed
Cusp of a craggy tooth.

Sipped and touched the nerve.

A tremor went through me as
Every cell felt: and I writhed.
Snow fell, and the leopard
Lies embalmed forever in ice.

But for the new life when it came,
The singing of the sun was unambiguous

KOBENA EYI ACQUAH

Africa Area Winner 1985 *The Man Who Died*

Kobena Eyi Acquah (born 1952) is from the Ewe people of Ghana. He has won several literary awards in his own country and is a past General Secretary of the Ghana Association of Writers. His poetry is wide-ranging in theme and technique, but much of it derives from the vigorous oral tradition of his background. *The Man Who Died* was a first book. Keta is a village in Eastern Ghana seriously eroded by the sea.

I Want to Go to Keta

I want to go to Keta
before it's washed away,
before the palm trees wither
and drown outside the bay.

I want to go to Keta
where boys drum all the day
and the girls dance *agbadza*
to keep the tears away.

I want to go to Keta
while yet they live who care
to point out like a star
that frothing spot out there

where they would sit with *dada*
those days the sea was land.
I want to go to Keta
while yet there's place to stand.

I want to go to Keta
before the tenderness
of grief so keen and bitter
chills to cold callousness

and the vagueness of laughter
drowns the shared joy of pain.
I want to go to Keta –
it might not long remain.

GARY GEDDES

Americas Area Winner 1985   *The Terracotta Army*

Gary Geddes (born 1940) is one of Canada's foremost poets. His
collections, in addition to the sequence of related character studies
which make up *The Terracotta Army*, include *Rivers Inlet, Snakeroot,
Letter of the Master of Horse, War Measures and other poems, The Acid
Test* and *Changes of State*. The army of the title refers to the terracotta
legions guarding the tomb of the First Emperor of China, discovered
by archaeologists in 1974.

Mess Sergeant

It was not so much the gossip that attracted me
to Bi's pottery, though there was plenty of that:

news of the latest atrocities against the people,
rights and property abolished, heads of children

staring vacantly from terraces, dismembered corpses
turning slowly in the current along the north bank

of the Wei. Rather it was a sort of clearing-house,
a confessional, where our greatest fears were exorcised

piecemeal through the barter of objective detail.
I remember the day when word came of the taking

of Yen. Streets ran with the colour of Ch'in's revenge.
The lute-player, Kao-Chien Li, who had plucked Ching K'o

on his way to assassinate the emperor, was blinded
and forced to serenade the victors without ceasing,

blood still running down his face and arms.
Not a sound was heard in the pottery, except the crackle

of logs burning and the sizzle of spit as the last
moisture escaped from the baking clay figures.

VIKRAM SETH

Asia Area Winner 1985   *The Humble Administrator's Garden*

Vikram Seth (born 1952) comes from Calcutta, India, though a large part of his education has been in Britain and the United States of America. *The Humble Administrator's Garden* was his second collection of poems, the first being published in Calcutta and entitled *Mappings*. *Mappings* focuses on the predicament of the Indian abroad, and it is worth noting that Seth has also written a travel book, *From Heaven Lake*, which is set in Tibet. (See also pp. 91-3.)

The Humble Administrator's Garden

A plump gold carp nudges a lily pad
And shakes the raindrops off like mercury,
And Mr Wang walks round. "Not bad, not bad."
He eyes the Fragrant Chamber dreamily.
He eyes the Rainbow Bridge. He may have got
The means by somewhat dubious means, but now
This is the loveliest of all gardens. What
Do scruples know of beauty anyhow?
The Humble Administrator admires a bee
Poised on a lotus, walks through the bamboo wood,
Strips half a dozen loquats off a tree
And looks about and sees that it is good.
   He leans against a willow with a dish
   And throws a dumpling to a passing fish.

MICHAEL LONGLEY

United Kingdom and Europe Area Winner 1985   *Poems 1963-83*

Michael Longley (born 1939) comes from Belfast, Northern Ireland, and is the author of many collections of poetry, including *No Continuing City, An Exploded View, Man Lying on a Wall,* and *The Echo Gate*. His poems are admired for their delicacy of perception and for their lyrical qualities, but often in the background the sounds of the political conflicts of Ulster can be heard.

The Linen Industry

Pulling up flax after the blue flowers have fallen
And laying our handfuls in the peaty water
To rot those grasses to the bone, or building stooks
That recall the skirts of an invisible dancer,

We become a part of the linen industry
And follow its processes to the grubby town
Where fields are compacted into window-boxes
And there is little room among the big machines.

But even in our attic under the skylight
We make love on a bleach green, the whole meadow
Draped with material turning white in the sun
As though snow reluctant to melt were our attire.

What's passion but a battering of stubborn stalks,
Then a gently combing out of fibres like hair
And a weaving of these into christening robes,
Into garments for a marriage or funeral?

Since it's like a bereavement once the labour's done
To find ourselves last workers in a dying trade,
Let flax be our matchmaker, our undertaker,
The provider of sheets for whatever the bed –

And be shy of your breasts in the presence of death,
Say that you look more beautiful in linen
Wearing white petticoats, the bow on your bodice
A butterfly attending the embroidered flowers.

NIYI OSUNDARE

Joint Winner 1986   *The Eye of the Earth*

Niyi Osundare (born 1947) is from Nigeria where, in addition to
academic work and writing, he has been responsible for a weekly
poetry column in a national newspaper. His collections of poetry
include *Songs of the Marketplace, Village Voices, A Nib in the Pond*
and *The Eye of the Earth*. His poems draw on the oral traditions of
his area of Nigeria near Ikere.

Raindrum

The roofs sizzle at the waking touch,
talkative like kettledrums
tightened by the iron fingers of drought

Streets break into liquid dance
gathering legs in the orchestra of the road
Streets break into liquid dance
gliding eloquently down the apron of the sky

A stray drop saunters down the thatch
of my remembrance
waking memories long dormant
under the dry leaves of time:

> of caked riverbeds
> and browned pastures
> of baking noons
> and grilling nights
> of earless cornfields
> and tired tubers

Then
Lightning strikes its match of rain
Barefoot, we tread the throbbing earth,

Renewed

Harvestcall

(To be chanted to lively bata *music)*

I

This is Iyanfoworogi
where, garnished in green
pounded yam rested its feted arms
on the back of stooping stakes.
This is Iyanfoworogi
where valiant heaps cracked, finally,
from the unquenchable zeal of fattening yams.

This is Iyanfoworogi
where yams, ripe and randy,
waged a noisy war against the knife;
here where, subbued by fire,
efuru* provoked mouthful clamour
from the combat of hungry wood:
>> the pestle fights the mortar
>> the mortar fights the pestle
>> a dough of contention smooths down
>> the rugged anger of hunger.

Here where yam wore the crown
in the reign of swollen roots
amid a retinue of vines and royal leaves;
between insistent sky and yielding earth,
the sun mellowed planting pageants
into harvest march,
a fiery pestle in his ripening hand.

This is Iyanfoworogi
where a tempting yam sauntered
out of the selling tray
and the marketplace became a mob
of instant suitors.

II

And this Oke Eniju
where coy cobs rocked lustily
in the loin of swaying stalks.

* *the king of yams*

Once here in May
a tasselled joy robed the field
like hemless green.
Once here in May
the sky was a riot of pollen grains
and ivory mills waited (im)patiently
for the browning of grey tassels.

And when June had finally grabbed the year
by her narrow waist
corn cobs flashed their milky teeth
in disrobing kitchens.
Plenty's season announced its coming
and the humming mill at dawn
suddenly became the village heart.

III

(Finally) Ogbese Odo
where cotton pods, lips duly parted
by December's sun,
draped busy farmsteads
in a harvest of smiles.
Here a blooming loom curtailed
the tiger claws of the harmattan
and earth's wardrobe lent a garb
to every season.

IV

(Music lowers in tempo, becoming solemn)

But where *are* they?
Where are they gone:
aroso, geregede, otiili, pakala†
which beckoned lustily to the reaping basket
Where are they
the yam pyramids which challenged the sun
in busy barns
Where are they
the pumpkins which caressed earthbreast
like mammary burdens
Where are they
the pods which sweetened harvest air
with the clutter of dispersing seeds?
Where are they? Where are they gone?

Uncountable seeds lie sleeping
in the womb of earth
uncountable seeds
awaiting the quickening tap
of our waking finger.

With our earth so warm
How can our hearth be so cold?

† *All four are types of beans.*

Dawncall

Come with me at dawn
When a matchless darkness couples earth and sky
And the world is one starless bed of frigid sweat
Come with me
When trees listen earlessly to the accent
Of the waking wind
Head-deep in the indigo of night.

Mark, oh mark this misty mob breaking out
Of the mouth of a yawning world
Swaddling the glowworm's winking lamps
On the inky poles of a sleepless fog.
Mark the young moon managing a milky flight
From the trumpet ambush of the first cock

Eyelids laden with dew, the grass cannot see the lines on its palm; puking like a baby, darkling, earth cannot count the fingers on her drowsy hand. Wet and wild the earth, where is the sun? Wet and wild how count the hands of the dozing clock behind the back of its solar face? Wet and wild the clock dissolved in dew. Dissolved. Tickless like a heart, ethered. Earth is timeless. Time less. And a termless halo surrounds our head havened in the firmament of reigning mist. Oh! that mob from earth's yawning mouth. Wet and wild a prancing *eusa** scuttles across dawn's corridor, its jaws a silent mill of hoarded kennels. Wet and wild the

* *Or okete, a nocturnal rodent.*

89

toad, tail-less like a forgetting race, leapless like a senile mountain. Wet and wild like a wind unwitched. Solitary hour wet and wild, solitary like an only finger, wild like a virgin brush. Solitary this hour, the earth swarmed by minds and matters, monsters and manikins. Solitary. And soulitary? A deafening silence usurps the earth. Silence in the leaping lair. Silence. Silence in the munching mill. Silence. Silence in conquerred covens. Silence.

Mark this misty mob breaking out
Of the mouth of a yawning earth
And this earthworm
Whose blood will break the fast of earth
When this dawn is done.

VIKRAM SETH

Joint Winner 1986   *The Golden Gate*

This is a novel in verse: thirteen sets of sonnets which concern the interlocking lives and relationships of a group of people in contemporary San Francisco. The excerpt that follows is a moment of authorial intervention, demonstrating Seth's virtuosity within his chosen form. (See also p. 84.)

5.1

A week ago, when I had finished
Writing the chapter you've just read
And with avidity undiminished
Was charting out the course ahead,
An editor – at a plush party
(Well-wined, -provisioned, speechy, hearty)
Hosted by (long live!) Thomas Cook
Where my Tibetan travel book
Was honored – seized my arm: "Dear fellow,
What's your next work?" "A novel . . ." "Great!
We hope that you, dear Mr Seth –"
". . . In verse," I added. He turned yellow.
"How marvellously quaint," he said,
And subsequently cut me dead.

5.2

Professor, publisher and critic
Each voiced his doubts. I felt misplaced.
A writer is a mere arthritic
Among these muscular Gods of Taste.
As for that sad blancmange, a poet –
The world is hard; he ought to know it.
Driveling in rhyme's all very well;
The question is, does spittle sell?
Since staggering home in deep depression,
My will's grown weak. My heart is sore.
My lyre is dumb. I have therefore
Convoked a morale-boosting session
With a few kind if doubtful friends
Who've asked me to explain my ends.

How do I justify this stanza?
These feminine rhymes? My wrinkled muse?
This whole passé extravaganza?
How can I (careless of time) use
The dusty bread molds of Onegin
In the brave bakery of Reagan?
The loaves will surely fail to rise
Or else go stale before my eyes.
The truth is, I can't justify it.
But as no shroud of critical terms
Can save my corpse from boring worms,
I may as well have fun and try it.
If it works, good; and if not, well
A theory won't postpone its knell.

Why, asks a friend, attempt tetrameter?
Because it once was noble, yet
Capers before the proud pentameter,
Tyrant of English. I regret
To see this marvelous swift meter
Demean its heritage, and peter
Into mere Hudibrastic tricks,
Unapostolic knacks and knicks.
But why take all this quite so badly?
I would not, had I world and time
To wait for reason, rhythm, rhyme
To reassert themselves, but sadly
The time is not remote when I
Will not be here to wait. That's why.

Reader, enough of this apology;
But spare me if I think it best,
Before I tether my monology,
To stake a stanza to suggest
You spend some unfilled day of leisure
By that original spring of pleasure:

Sweet-watered, fluent, clear, light, blithe
(This homage merely pays a tithe
Of what in joy and inspiration
It gave me once and does not cease
To give me) – Pushkin's masterpiece
In Johnston's luminous translation:
Eugene Onegin – like champagne
Its effervescence stirs my brain.

VICKI RAYMOND

Best first-time published poet 1986   *Holiday Girls and Other Poems*

Vicki Raymond (born 1949) is Australian, from the state of Victoria, and has worked for several years in the Australian High Commission in London. Since winning the prize, she has taken part in many poetry readings in the UK and Europe.

Holiday Girls

"British Holiday Girls in Death Crash"
– newspaper headline.

Let Beryl Cook paint this triptych. First,
the Setting Out from Victoria. Laden
with overnight bags and make-up cases,
they jostle on to the train. Their summer dresses
patterned with daisies, shoulders bare
in expectation of bronze, their "natural" perms
guaranteed to last through swimming pool and disco,
mark them out from the business crowd.
That guard at the gate with his back toward us:
is that a hand of bones stretched out
to take the ticket? Too late to look now.

The middle panel, the Death Crash, should show
a blackened plain under a bloody sky,
and strewn on the plain, in tender enumeration,
squashed lipsticks, bottles oozing white pulp
of lotions, Instamatics, Mars bars,
Mills and Boon romances, and the Holiday Girls:
the legs of one sticking out from under
some piece of machinery, the other seen
in outline only, under the ambulance sheet.

And last, the Arrival at Butlin's, Death-on-Sea.
A three-piece band of tuxedoed angels strikes up:
their haloes are inscribed "Kiss Me Quick" and "You've Had It".
Down from the neon-lit Pleasure Pavilion pours
the army of saints and martyrs, displaying
the symbols and instruments of their suffering:
Auntie May with her surgical stockings, Uncle Ted
with his x-ray plates, and cousin George,
clutching the steering shaft that went through his chest.

94

And after them, the Thousand Virgins (half a dozen
will do, we must imagine the rest),
each one a Miss Lovely Legs, and, in their midst,
holding a tray of rock cakes, our Heavenly Mum.

Now let the eye travel upward. Be bold, Mrs Cook,
to paint what the heart of the poor has always known:
the Son setting out the cups and saucers for tea,
the Father in braces and rolled-up trousers
coming up from the sea, and a shimmering bird
nourished by no earthly cuttlefish, spreading its wings
over the strapless shoulders and permanent curls
of the laugh-a-minute, whew-what-a-scorcher,
British death-crash, sic-transit-Bank-Holiday-Monday,
Holiday Girls.

The Witch Sycorax Addresses Her Lover

Perhaps you were thinking of leaving.
Don't try. You see, while you were asleep,
I stole some hair from you. It's buried –
where, I won't say – and it will tighten
round your throat and draw you back to me,
or choke your life out while you're sleeping.

Perhaps you fancy someone else:
if so, I have bad news for you.
There is a candle one can make,
obscene in shape, not made of wax
but something else – I won't say what.
As it melts, so melts your manhood.

Perhaps you are bored with me.
Here is a nice black milkshake,
will make you play the satyr.
Come: that is only a branch
scraping the window. Nothing
can harm you. I'm here. Relax.

IAIN CRICHTON SMITH

United Kingdom and Europe Area Winner 1986   *A Life*

Iain Crichton Smith (born 1928) published his first collection of poems in English in 1955. His prolific output includes novels, stories and plays, as well as poems in both English and Gaelic. *A Life* is his verse autobiography, beginning on the island of Lewis, and takes the poet to Aberdeen University, through National Service to Oban and Taynuilt, where he now lives.

Aberdeen University 1945-49: I

The glitter of the water and the wake . . .
Heading for University in Aberdeen.
It's an autumn morning. I am seventeen.
Above the Isle of Skye the dawn's a flag

of red infuriate ore. I see the train
for the first time ever steaming from the Kyle
beyond the screaming seagulls, in the smell
of salt and herring. There's a tall sad crane.

The landscape, rich, harmonious, unwinds
its perfect symmetry: not the barren stone
and vague frail fences I have always known.
I hold my Homer steady in my hand.

All day we travel and at last dismount
at the busy station of that sparkling town.
A beggar with black glasses sitting down
on the hard stone holds out his cap. I count

the pennies in it. Should I freely give?
Or being more shameful than himself refrain?
His definite shadow is the day's black stain.
How in such open weakness learn to live?

I turn away, the money in my hand,
profusely sweating, in that granite blaze.
Unknown, unlooked at, I pick up my case.
Everything's glittering and transient.

LORNA GOODISON

Americas Area Winner 1986   *I Am Becoming My Mother*

Lorna Goodison (born 1947) grew up in Kingston, and studied art in Jamaica and New York. *I Am Becoming My Mother* is her second book of poetry, following *Tamarind Season*. She has illustrated both collections herself. Lorna Goodison's poetry is much concerned with what it means to be a woman and a writer. She lives in Jamaica and has taught there and in America.

"Mine, O thou Lord of life, send my roots rain"

– Gerard Manley Hopkins

For I've been planted long
in a sere dry place
watered only occasionally
with odd overflows
from a passing cloud's face.
In my morning
I imitated the bougainvillaea
(in appearances
I'm hybrid)
I gave forth defiant alleluias
of flowering
covered my aridity with
red petalled blisters
grouped close, from far
they were a borealis of
save-face flowers.
In the middle of my
life span
my trunk's not so limber
my sap flows thicker
my region has posted signs
that speak of scarce water.
At night God, I feel
my feet powder.
Lord let the preying worms
wait to feast in vain.
In this noon of my orchard
send me deep rain.

ANDREW TAYLOR

Australia and Pacific Area Winner 1986   *Travelling*

Andrew Taylor (born 1940) is from the Australian state of Victoria.
He teaches English at Adelaide University. His previous books of
poetry include *The Cool Change, Ice Fishing, The Invention of Fire,
The Cat's Chin and Ears, Parabolas,* and *Selected Poems: 1960-1980.*

Nature
for David Malouf

Nature isn't enough. Those
little lines of sportive wood run wild
deny our taste for history
and good cooking. Not surprising then
Australia discovered, untouched
by European hands, was the final
poverty, the ideal outpost
for His Majesty's outcasts.

Even today, after the ploughs and axes,
nature untouched, lovely though she may be
and hard to find and harder still
really to see, scent or hear, rejects us.
She's what we aren't, and the green slopes
of European woodland speak a tongue
more baffling than Gothic or the wild brogue
full of leaves, hanging gods and cattle
that troubled Tacitus. They brood
with a vegetative thoroughness
that excludes us. They are Europe
before Europeans, and we hurry
down freeways, fearful that trees
might close their arms, grass
swallow the tarmac and the exits choke
with lantana and blackberries.

Deserts speak for God, who is male
dictatorial and builds in stone. God
wants us, nature doesn't. She's fighting for
her earth, to heal the scars, cars gone
and us too.
                    Nature, not *victrix* then

but held at bay, subversive,
the underground activist, thrusting
handfuls of daisies from the cracks
of ducal ramparts, spreading
a luminous carpet of couch
in the shade of a tankstand, and these
festoons of capers on the walls
of Campagnatico, favours us best.

Epilogue

I have crossed an ocean
I have lost my tongue
from the root of the old
one
a new one has sprung

GRACE NICHOLS

Acknowledgements

e editor and publishers gratefully acknowledge permission to reprint
ems in this anthology. Every effort has been made to trace copyright
lders; the publishers would be pleased to hear from any not acknow-
lged.

inua Achebe: from *Beware, Soul Brother,* originally published by
Nwafime Publishers Limited, Nigeria, 1971; Heinemann Educational
Books Limited, London, 1971. Reprinted by permission of the pub-
ishers.

bena Eyi Acquah: from *The Man Who Died,* Asempa Publishers, Accra,
Ghana, 1984. Reprinted by permission of the author and publishers.

noshenko Aslanides: from *The Greek Connection,* published by the
author in Canberra, Australia, 1977.

ayne Brown: from *On the Coast,* André Deutsch Limited, London,
1972. Reprinted by permission of the publishers.

vid Dabydeen: from *Slave Song,* Dangeroo Press, Denmark, 1984.
Reprinted by permission of the publishers.

aris Edmond: from *Selected Poems,* Oxford University Press, New
Zealand, 1984. Reprinted by permission of the author and publishers.

ry Geddes: from *The Terracotta Army,* Oberon Press, Ottawa, Canada,
1986. Reprinted by permission of the publishers.

er Goldsworthy: from *Readings from Ecclesiastes,* Angus & Robertson
Publishers, 1982. Reprinted by permission of the publishers.

na Goodison: from *I Am Becoming My Mother,* New Beacon Books
Limited, London, 1986. Reprinted by permission of the publishers.

vin Hart: from *The Departure,* University of Queensland Press, Aus-
ralia, 1978. Reprinted by permission of the publishers.

nothy Holmes: from *Double Element,* Wordsmiths Zambia Limited,
985. Reprinted by permission of the author.

hael Jackson: from *Latitudes of Exile,* John McIndoe Limited, Dunedin,
New Zealand, 1976. Reprinted by permission of the author and pub-
shers.

er Kocan: from *The Other Side of the Fence,* University of Queensland
Press, Australia, 1975. Reprinted by permission of the publishers.

n Kolatkar: from *Jejuri,* Clearing House, Bombay, India, 1976. Re-
rinted by permission of the author.

101

Shirley Lim: from *Crossing the Peninsula and Other Poems*, Heineman Educational Books (Asia) Limited, Singapore, 1980. Reprinted b permission of the author.

Audrey Longbottom: from *Relatives and Reliques*, Wentworth Books P Limited, Surry Hills, Australia, 1979.

Michael Longley: from *Poems 1963-83*, The Salamander Press, Edinburg and The Gallery Press, Dublin, 1984. Reprinted by permission of th author

George McWhirter: from *Catalan Poems*, Oberon Press, Ottawa, Canad 1971. Reprinted by permission of the publishers.

David Mitchell: from *Pipe Dreams in Ponsonby*, Stephen Chan, Aucklan New Zealand, 1972; reprinted by Caveman Press, 1975.

Grace Nichols: from *I is a long memoried woman*, Karnak House, Londo 1983. Reprinted by permission of the publishers.

Richard Ntiru: from *Tensions*, East African Publishing House Limite Nairobi, Kenya, 1971. Reprinted by permission of the author and pu lishers.

Gabriel Okara: from *The Fisherman's Invocation*, Ethiope Publishir Corporation, Benin City, Nigeria and Heinemann Educational Boo Limited, London, 1978. Reprinted by permission of the publishers

Niyi Osundare: from *The Eye of the Earth*, Heinemann Educational Boo (Nigeria) Limited, 1986.

Rajagopal Parthasarathy: from *Rough Passage*, © Oxford University Pres India, 1977. Reprinted by permission of Oxford University Press.

Vicki Raymond: from *Holiday Girls and Other Poems*, Twelvetrees Pu lishing Company, Tasmania, Australia, 1986. Reprinted by permissio of the publishers.

Philip Salom: from *The Silent Piano*, Freemantle Arts Centre Press, Au tralia, 1980. Reprinted by permission of the publishers.

Dennis Scott: from *Uncle Time*, University of Pittsburgh Press, US. © 1973 by Dennis Scott. Reprinted by permission of the publisher

Vikram Seth: from *The Humble Administrator's Garden*, Carcanet Pres Manchester, 1985. Reprinted by permission of the publishers. Fro *The Golden Gate*, © Faber and Faber, London; Random House In New York, 1986. Reprinted by permission of both publishers.

Iain Crichton Smith: from *A Life*, Carcanet Press, Manchester, 198 Reprinted by permission of the publishers.

Andrew Taylor: from *Travelling*, University of Queensland Press, Au tralia, 1986. Reprinted by permission of the publishers.

Robin Thurston: from *Believed Dangerous*, University of Queensland Press, Australia, 1975. Reprinted by permission of the publishers.

Brian Turner: from *Ladders of Rain*, John McIndoe Limited, Dunedin, New Zealand, 1978. Reprinted by permission of the publishers.

Geoffrey Ursell: from *Trap Lines*, Turnstone Press, Winnipeg, Canada, 1982. Reprinted by permission of the publishers.

POETRY
Signatures

llian Clarke, *Selected Poems*   0 85635 594 1

. record the changes economic collapse is bringing to Wales, memories
a journey through France, fruit, flowers and work in the fields. . . . the
ems are richly satisfying, accumulating like bottled fruit gleaming
ong a pantry shelf.' – *Stand*

onald Davie, *Selected Poems*   0 85635 595 X

avie is an exciting poet because he takes nothing for granted, and
cause he takes risks . . . making sense and making whole, as and
erever he can.' – *Guardian*

D. Hope, *Selected Poems*   0 85635 640 9

e first Australian to make a name outside his homeland, Hope is one
the finest poets writing in English . . . this well-made selection shows
pe pursuing truth and reason in the richest and most resonant lan-
age.' – *Observer*

zabeth Jennings, *Selected Poems*   0 85635 282 9

e conveys a sense of something hidden but powerfully alive in her;
e may be the last poet of what used to be called the soul. . . . She is
e of the few living poets one could not do without.' – *Spectator*

McMillan, *Selected Poems*   0 85635 718 9

are poems of their time; they share a cool obliquity with Elvis Cos-
o's songs, Glen Baxter's cartoons . . . but they do not pander to their
e, . . . exploiting language's ambiguous malfunctions and unexpected
al quirks.' – *Times Literary Supplement*

vin Morgan, *Selected Poems*   0 85635 596 8

combine verbal inventiveness and formal innovation . . . at the same
e he luminously communicates the power and delight of the ordi-
y.' – *Times Literary Supplement*

A. Murray, *Selected Poems*   0 85635 667 0

A. Murray is an Australian, a waterfall of a poet, satisfying as a
ight of Coonawarra Cabernet – a year's discovery.' – *Guardian*

Iain Crichton Smith, *Selected Poems* 0 85635 597

'...an indubitably inspired poet, taking on the world in poem after poem.' – *The Times*

Jeffrey Wainwright, *Selected Poems* 0 85635 598

'...his uncanny ability to voice the feelings of the oppressed and dissenting and thus to range from...domestic intimacy to visionary fervour has already made his historical cycles minor classics.' – *Sunday Times*

Sylvia Townsend Warner, *Selected Poems* 0 85635 585

'Anyone thinking that wit, penetration...an enduring and exact delight in the natural world, all united with absolute integrity, are as needed as they are rare, would do well to read [Sylvia Townsend Warner's poems].' – *Observer*

Andrew Waterman, *Selected Poems* 0 85635 668

'...a highly intelligent poet [who lectures at the New University of Ulster] for whom the troubles are, in every sense, on the doorstep, and his *Selected Poems* is an impressive volume.' – *Encounter*

Robert Wells, *Selected Poems* 0 85635 669

'He is a scholar familiar with Virgil and Theocritus; he has also worked as a farm hand...his acute sense of physical presence extends at once to areas at once physiological and psychological...He is undoubtedly a poet.' – *London Review of Books*

FyfieldBooks

"The Fyfield Books series provides an admirable service in pub-
lishing good inexpensive selections from the works of interesting
but neglected poets"

– British Book News

THOMAS LOVELL BEDDOES (1803-49)
Selected Poems
edited by Judith Higgens

THE BRONTË SISTERS
Selected Poems
edited by Stevie Davies

ELIZABETH BARRETT BROWNING (1806-61)
Selected Poems
edited by Malcolm Hicks

THOMAS CAMPION (1567-1620)
Ayres and Observations
edited by Joan Hart

GEORGE CHAPMAN (?1559-1634)
Selected Poems
edited by Eirean Wain

THOMAS CHATTERTON (1752-70)
Selected Poems
edited by Grevel Lindop

ARTHUR HUGH CLOUGH (1819-1861)
Selected Poems
edited by Shirley Chew

CHARLES COTTON (1630-87)
Selected Poems
edited by Ken Robinson

WILLIAM COWPER (1731-1800)
Selected Poems
edited by Nick Rhodes

GEORGE CRABBE (1754-1832)
Selected Poems
edited by Jem Poster

MICHAEL DRAYTON (1563-1631)
Selected Poems
edited by Vivian Thomas

GEORGE GASCOIGNE (1530-77)
The Green Knight:
selected poems and prose
edited by Roger Pooley

JOHN GAY (1685-1732)
Selected Poems
edited by Marcus Walsh

JOHN GOWER (1330-1408)
Selected Poetry
edited by Carole Weinberg

THOMAS GRAY (1716-71)
Selected Poems
edited by John Heath-Stubbs

ROBERT HENRYSON (1425?-1508?)
Selected Poems
edited by W.R.J. Barron

ROBERT HERRICK (1591-1674)
Selected Poems
edited by David Jesson-Dibley

THOMAS HOCCLEVE (1348-1430)
Selected Poems
edited by Bernard O'Donoghue

BEN JONSON (1572-1637)
Epigrams & The Forest
edited by Richard Dutton

WALTER SAVAGE LANDOR (1775-1864)
Selected Poems and Prose
edited by Keith Hanley

RICHARD LOVELACE (1618-1657/8)
Selected Poems
edited by Gerald Hammond

ANDREW MARVELL (1621-78)
Selected Poems
edited by Bill Hutchings

GEORGE MEREDITH (1828-1909)
Selected Poems
edited by Keith Hanley

CHARLES OF ORLEANS (1394-1465)
Selected Poems
edited by Sally Purcell

SIR WALTER RALEGH (?1554-1618)
Selected Writings
edited by Gerald Hammond

JOHN WILMOT, EARL OF ROCHESTER
(1648-80)
The Debt to Pleasure
edited by John Adlard

CHRISTINA ROSSETTI (1830-94)
Selected Poems
edited by C.H. Sisson

SIR PHILIP SIDNEY (1554-86)
Selected Writings
edited by Richard Dutton

JOHN SKELTON (1460-1529)
Selected Poems
edited by Gerald Hammond

CHRISTOPHER SMART (1722-71)
Selected Poems
edited by Marcus Walsh

DONALD STANFORD (editor)
Three poets of the Rhymers' Cl
Lionel Johnson, Ernest Dowson
John Davidson

HENRY HOWARD, EARL OF SURREY
(1517-47)
Selected Poems
edited by Dennis Keene

JONATHAN SWIFT (1667-1745)
Selected Poems
edited by C.H. Sisson

ALGERNON CHARLES SWINBURNE
(1837-1909)
Selected Poems
edited by L.M. Findlay

ARTHUR SYMONS (1865-1945)
Selected Writings
edited by R.V. Holdsworth

THOMAS TRAHERNE (?1637-74)
Selected Writings
edited by Dick Davis

HENRY VAUGHAN (1622-95)
Selected Poems
edited by Robert B. Shaw

ANNE FINCH, COUNTESS OF WINCHILS
(1661-1720)
Selected Poems
edited by Denys Thompson

EDWARD YOUNG (1683-1765)
Selected Poems
edited by Brian Hepworth

"Carcanet are doing an excellent job in this series: the editio
are labours of love, not just commercial enterprises. I hope th
are familiar to all readers and teachers of literature."
— *Times Literary Suppleme*